●= MAKE YOUR TRAINING RESULTS LAST

A Practical Guide To Successful Training Follow-Through

Gloria E. Bader

Audrey E. Bloom

Richard Chang Associates, Inc.
Publications Division
Irvine, California

MAKE YOUR TRAINING RESULTS LAST

A Practical Guide To Successful Training Follow-Through

Gloria E. Bader
Audrey E. Bloom

Library of Congress Catalog Card Number
94-68224

© 1994, Richard Chang Associates, Inc.
Printed in the United States of America

ISBN 1-883553-39-3

Second printing November 1995

Richard Chang Associates, Inc.
Publications Division
41 Corporate Park, Suite 230
Irvine, CA 92714
(800) 756-8096 • Fax (714) 756-0853

Acknowledgments

About The Authors

Gloria E. Bader is President of The Bader Group, a San Diego-based management consulting firm specializing in leadership, communication, customer service, and teamwork. She is a popular lecturer at San Diego State University's School of Business and an executive coach at the Center for Creative Leadership.

Audrey E. Bloom is a freelance instructional designer with a Masters degree in Educational Technology from San Diego State University. She researches and develops training materials on a wide range of technical and management topics.

The authors would like to acknowledge the support of the entire team of professionals at Richard Chang Associates, Inc. for their contribution to the guidebook development process. In addition, special thanks are extended to the many client organizations who have helped us shape the practical ideas and proven methods shared in this guidebook.

Additional Credits

Editors: Sarah Ortlieb Fraser and Ruth Stingley

Reviewers: P. Keith Kelly and Pamela Wade

Graphic Layout: Christina Slater

Cover Design: John Odam Design Associates

PREFACE

The 1990's have already presented individuals and organizations with some very difficult challenges to face and overcome. So who will have the advantage as we move toward the year 2000 and beyond?

The advantage will belong to those with a commitment to continuous learning. Whether on an individual basis or as an entire organization, one key ingredient to building a continuous learning environment is *The Practical Guidebook Collection* brought to you by the Publications Division of Richard Chang Associates, Inc.

After understanding the future *"learning needs"* expressed by our clients and other potential customers, we are pleased to publish *The Practical Guidebook Collection*. These guidebooks are designed to provide you with proven, *"real-world"* tips, tools, and techniques— on a wide range of subjects—that you can apply in the workplace and/or on a personal level immediately.

Once you've had a chance to benefit from *The Practical Guidebook Collection*, please share your feedback with us. We've included a brief *Evaluation and Feedback Form* at the end of the guidebook that you can fax to us at (714) 756-0853.

With your feedback, we can continuously improve the resources we are providing through the Publications Division of Richard Chang Associates, Inc.

Wishing you successful reading,

Richard Y. Chang
President and CEO
Richard Chang Associates, Inc.

TABLE OF CONTENTS

"Apply yourself. Get all the education you can, but then, by God, do something. Don't just stand there, make it happen."

Lee Iacocca

CHAPTER ONE

INTRODUCTION

Why Read This Guidebook?

Everything is changing. New management initiatives abound. Customer service focus. Safety in the workplace. Quality improvement. Computer technology and new software programs. Employee involvement. The supervisor as coach. Cultural diversity. Empowerment. Teams.

Many organizations provide training in these topics with the expectation that employee participants will return from the class, workshop, or seminar with new ideas and attitudes. Organizations spend countless hours and millions of dollars in training every year.

One manager, Maurice, noticed that three members of his print shop staff were complaining about demanding customers and speaking abruptly to them. He decided to send them to a seminar called *Powerful Customer Service* to improve their attitudes. The seminar was informative and motivational, but afterwards Maurice noticed only minor improvements in the way the staff worked with customers.

After a week, Maurice heard one staff member make rude excuses to a customer about a late order. Obviously, the glow of the seminar was lost. Called the *spray and pray* approach, this kind of training does not last.

Maurice was frustrated. He didn't realize that he had to plan for, and follow-through on, the ideas presented in the customer service seminar. His investment of a day's wages for his three people at a six-hour seminar was virtually wasted. *(Maurice wanted to continue staff training).* He also planned to attend a ten-part management development program offered through a local business group.

By applying the tools and techniques of this guidebook, Maurice can greatly improve the value and impact of his— and the staff's—training.

The demand for good training programs covering the changing topics important to business will never go away. Neither will the expense; so it is important that training programs have a lasting effect and that every training dollar counts.

Training must make a difference and help your organization reach its goals. It must encourage and guide new ways of doing business. When the evaluation form is collected at the end of the program and training has been linked to measurable results, the training is not over—it is just beginning. This guidebook offers a new approach to training and powerful ways to learn in organizations.

Make Your Training Results Last assumes that you have conducted a good needs analysis and discovered the particular skills, behaviors, or information required for business success. This guidebook also assumes that a manager or training professional has strongly recommended a training program. From there, this guidebook provides practical suggestions for fostering lasting success.

Who Should Read This Guidebook?

Make Your Training Results Last offers managers, like Maurice, tools and techniques to stretch their training dollars and guarantee the effectiveness of programs. If you are sending your staff to an organization-wide training program or to outside seminars, you can double the return on your investment by implementing the ideas suggested in this guidebook.

Your organization's training staff will benefit from the course design, planning, and preparation tips in *Make Your Training Results Last*. Facilitators or trainers will increase their understanding of, and commitment to, goal setting and follow-through coaching of trainees.

Human Resource departments will also benefit from this guidebook's suggestions on how to tie training objectives to performance appraisals, rewards, and motivational efforts. As a training participant, you can make the most of the training opportunities your organization provides by using the ideas presented here. If you are part of a work team, you will learn new ways to evaluate training programs before you spend time and money on them.

When And How To Use It

Use this guidebook as you begin the process of developing or selecting a training program. Effective training begins long before the classroom is reserved and the workbooks are printed. The best way to ensure powerful results from training is to build in a commitment to training follow-through from the start.

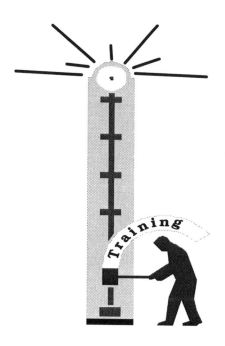

Perhaps you are familiar with the traditional model for designing training programs, which covers needs assessment, design, development, delivery, and evaluation. Is something missing? Yes—there is usually no follow-through phase. But follow-through is critically important in the learning process, just as it is in marksmanship, tennis, and many other sports. Although we have positioned it at the end of the High-IMPACT Training™ Model in Chapter Four, you will discover in this guidebook that follow-through starts at the beginning.

The case examples, checklists, planning charts, and lists of suggestions presented in this guidebook will make it easy for anyone involved in training to implement programs that last and build trainee confidence and skills.

Make use of this guidebook as you develop a training program to prompt your consideration of follow-through strategies. Facilitators can use the proven tips in this guidebook during the actual training event, whether it is a one-hour talk on safety or a 40-hour course on quality improvement.

If you plan to purchase a complete training package or contract an outside organization for training help, you will benefit from the checklist on how to select, buy, and implement powerful training courses. You will also find suggestions on interviewing and contracting training professionals.

Apply the techniques of this guidebook at the conclusion of a workshop to remind you of opportunities for follow-through. After the training program, the manager, training facilitator, and participants can continue to grow and nurture the learning that took place through this guidebook's suggestions.

Before you meet the players in the case examples that follow, you will want to understand what it takes to create lasting results, the broad view of training, and the importance of a learning environment.

CHAPTER TWO

WHAT IT TAKES TO CREATE LASTING RESULTS

Defining Training Follow-Through

Training follow-through includes the steps an organization, department, manager, or trainee takes before, during, and after a training program to ensure that the benefits of training last. When training follow-through occurs, trainees actually apply the principles, skills, behaviors, and information learned during the program. Thus, the training effort makes a difference.

Follow-through creates conditions that refine and reinforce the workshop or course content. The specific steps and conditions change with each training topic, but key ground rules exist. Begin by taking a broader view of your organization.

The Broader View

Commitment to training results starts with the basic values and culture of your organization. The following four questions will help you determine the readiness of your organization to make training benefits last.

1. **Are the goals of my organization clear?**
   As directly as possible, you want to tie the training objectives and topics to these goals and to the performance required of trainees. If the training objectives become part of the trainee's performance measures, the training will have significant impact.

2. **Does my organization value improvement?**
   Look for signs. For example, do people feel encouraged to try new things and to learn? You also need tolerance for the kinds of mistakes beginners usually make.

3. **Does the training budget survive even tough times?**
   Increasing the impact of a training program requires time and dollars beyond the cost of purchasing or designing a program. The actual follow-through work often takes longer than the training program itself.

4. **Who is accountable for training results?**
   You will want to consult with this person about his or her goals and commitment to follow-through. You might need to take this responsibility on yourself.

The Learning Environment

What happens after people from your organization return from a training class? What kind of energy do they have? What do they talk about? Do they share new ideas and examples at a staff meeting? Do they circulate course materials for others to see? Do they practice new ways of doing things? Do you see changes? A positive answer to each of these questions indicates a strong learning environment.

When individuals become comfortable with their new behaviors and skills, and when performance improvement is evident, others are encouraged to participate in similar training opportunities. The excitement of learning and making positive changes motivates others.

In addition to having a strong learning environment, organizations that make training results last have other useful tools and systems in place. For example, some include training goals and outcomes in performance reviews; others tie recognition and rewards to training success, and many have books, videos, or audiotapes available to supplement training.

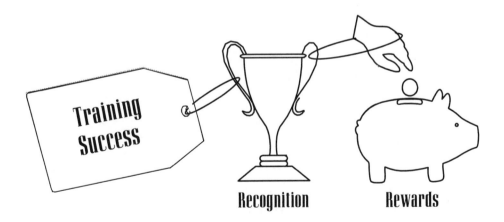

Recognition   Rewards

Obstacles

Knowing your organization's obstacles to effective follow-through will help you plan wisely to reduce or overcome them. Possible obstacles include trainees' motivation, time constraints, the manager's skills, poor timing, and lack of resources.

Motivation

If attendance at a workshop or seminar is mandatory, you have probably not thought through the motivational component of training. Training of hostages has little hope of follow-through. Unmotivated trainees have not answered the question, *"What are the benefits in it for me?"*

Too often, the purpose of training is unclear. Organizations ask trainees to attend a particular training session without understanding the benefits, and without goals or preparation.

Time constraints

 Day-to-day crises and demands prevent organizations from following-through on training events. Trainees returning to their jobs have missed work hours, days, or weeks, and are pressed to catch up. Occasionally, there is lack of support from trainers and facilitators who don't have time to assist the trainees once the program is completed.

One organization presented a day-long course on coaching skills for managers and team leaders without planning for follow-through or practice afterwards. A better plan offers a four-hour course followed *(within several days)* by a three-hour on-the-job application session, and a one-hour feedback session with the training staff. Participants schedule this application time in advance of the training. This type of creative program design lets the training staff spend more time guiding the trainees and building their confidence. In such cases, learned skills are more likely to last.

The manager's skills

A manager's lack of coaching skills is another critical barrier to application of training. She may not be available, capable, or willing to observe performance back on the job and provide constructive feedback. She may not realize that people need reinforcement as they try out new behaviors.

Or, the manager herself may not practice the behaviors or techniques presented in the training program. When a recent trainee sees his manager acting differently from the new ways learned, confusion results, discouragement sets in, and the new behaviors discontinue.

Timing

Timing is everything. Scheduling the training program too far in advance of the skill application or use of the information limits the value of the training. Scheduling training too close to the time when the skills are needed may not allow enough time for practice. One organization conducted a three-day workshop to introduce Continuous Quality Improvement principles without a plan to launch problem-solving teams right away.

Lack of resources

Frequently, a lack of physical space or equipment hinders follow-through on particular training subjects. A spreadsheet computer training course requires the proper software and tools so that the trainee can practice and use the  spreadsheet right away. No matter how effective an interviewing skills course, a manager must have a private place to conduct interviews for full implementation of the course content.

The Players

Manager

The manager wears many hats in today's organizations. She serves as a project manager, a technical resource, a customer relations expert, and a coach for her employees.

Motivating   **Training**   **Evaluating**

The coaching role most directly relates to lasting training results. It includes motivating staff, training them, and evaluating their performance. A manager who has other training resources available within an organization is fortunate. Yet, she cannot delegate the responsibility for ensuring the results of others' training. Prior to a training event, managers need to allocate time on their calendars to coach and conduct follow-through activities.

Training staff

Many organizations have a one-person training department. This individual is responsible for doing it all *(e.g., locating resource materials, writing, scheduling, and presenting various programs)*. Other organizations have large staffs of training specialists, writers, and facilitators. Training products are often purchased from vendors who specialize in a particular topic. Sometimes a training consultant is hired to develop or present a workshop or seminar. In each of these cases, plan and implement solid training follow-through activities.

Trainees

Trainees who want to learn and practice the new skills or behaviors create training results through their own motivation. If the trainee is well-prepared, understands the purpose of the training program, and sees a benefit to himself, he will not say, *"I was sent. What is this all about?"*

The Commitment To Follow-Through

An analogy

You've just purchased several new, vigorous ivy plants from the local nursery. You bring the containers home, eager to plant them.

Your follow-through choices are:

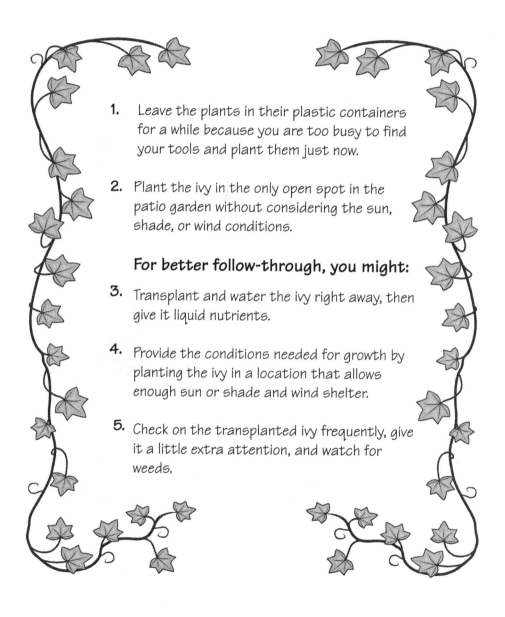

1. Leave the plants in their plastic containers for a while because you are too busy to find your tools and plant them just now.

2. Plant the ivy in the only open spot in the patio garden without considering the sun, shade, or wind conditions.

For better follow-through, you might:

3. Transplant and water the ivy right away, then give it liquid nutrients.

4. Provide the conditions needed for growth by planting the ivy in a location that allows enough sun or shade and wind shelter.

5. Check on the transplanted ivy frequently, give it a little extra attention, and watch for weeds.

Sending staff to a training program without a commitment to follow-through is like making one of the first two choices on the previous page. A commitment to follow-through after a training program is similar to making one or more of the last three choices.

The most difficult part of a course or workshop is the day after the program. The trainee returns to the procedures, coworkers, and sights and sounds of the familiar work environment. Phones ring and deadlines push us into old habits. Like the new ivy plant that remains unattended for too long in its original container, the training notebooks are shelved.

Successful training begins with a commitment to applying it. The design and delivery of excellent training provides tools to encourage and motivate the trainee long after the program itself. Let's meet some managers, training staff, and trainees who really want to cultivate learning and lasting results.

CHAPTER THREE

TWO ORGANIZATIONS EXPERIENCE TWO PROGRAMS

Helene And Kami At Arrow Computer

Arrow Computer is a young, fast-growing organization that encourages innovation and experimentation to improve quality and speed. Arrow places a high value on training. The organization includes expectations for ongoing learning in every employee's job description. Progress on training goals is discussed during every employee's annual performance review.

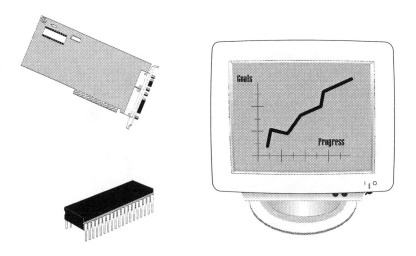

Helene manages a busy circuit board manufacturing and service department for Arrow. Her staff of eight technicians keeps a hectic pace and handles frequent, tight deadlines. They must constantly focus on the tasks of each day. Customers often want repair service within 24 hours, and generally the staff responds well to these demands. Helene's staff is always open to new ways of doing business and learning from each other. From time to time, Helene enlists the help of Kami, the organization's training specialist.

Recently, Kami sent Helene a brochure about a highly recommended customer service training program. The program's brochure contains a number of endorsements from well-known organizations and a short demonstration video. The four-hour customer service workshop, entitled *Meeting Customer Needs Through Quality*, is taught by Mario, a marketing consultant and author of a popular book on building customer relationships.

The usual workshop combines a presentation, a 15-minute video, and small group activities. Trainees receive a 30-page workbook that includes copies of some of the overhead transparencies, several short articles, and worksheets for the activities.

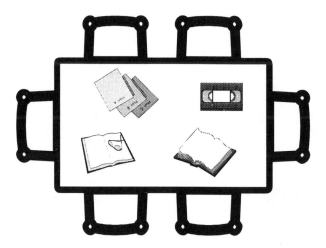

Mario's office sends his clients a short questionnaire two weeks in advance of the scheduled workshop so he can learn more about their businesses and customers. However, his program is basically the same for every audience. There are usually 50 to 70 participants in each session. Because these are large audiences, there is little opportunity for individual questions or discussions with the instructor.

A course on meeting effectiveness, *Making Our Meetings More Productive,* is also scheduled on Arrow's upcoming training calendar. Kami has offered to deliver the four, two-hour sessions on planning and facilitating group meetings to Helene's department. The course covers agenda-building, group dynamics, and group decision-making tools.

This meeting effectiveness program was originally developed by the training staff at Kami's former organization, Mountain Health. Seeing the need for a similar program at Arrow Computer, Kami requested and received permission to offer the same course at Arrow, using slightly modified examples.

An important feature of the program design is the series of project assignments required of participants between each session.

Jim And Charlene At Mountain Health

Jim is the manager of a large, home health care group. It is a fast-growing division within a large hospital and medical services organization called Mountain Health. Jim directs 12 area supervisors who schedule, supervise, and train more than 75 full- and part-time nurses and nursing aides. The number of home health visits and services has tripled over the last few years and Jim's staff must constantly adjust to increased workloads, new techniques and procedures.

The professional nursing staff enjoys their independence as they administer complex medications and treatments in patients' homes. They truly believe in the value of home care and are dedicated to maintaining high professional standards.

Mountain Health's large training department is also interested in Mario's *Meeting Customer Needs Through Quality* training program. Charlene is one of the department's three training managers. Since the home health nurses and supervisors cannot all leave the field at once, Charlene arranges for Mario to present to half of the group in the morning and the other half in the afternoon. Clinical staff members from other divisions also plan to attend each session.

Charlene plans to present Mountain Health's original course, *Making Our Meetings More Productive*, to the twelve supervisors on Jim's staff.

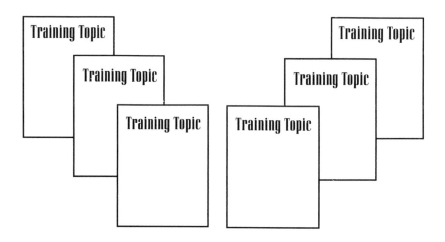

Helene and Kami *(Arrow Computer)*, and Jim and Charlene *(Mountain Health)*, have identified important training topics for their organizations. As the following chapters demonstrate, they realize that good training results require a training program design that begins well before, and extends long after, the actual delivery of the seminar or workshop.

The Players At A Glance		
Organization and Department/ Division	Arrow Computer Circuit Board Manufacturing and Service Department	Mountain Health Home Health Care Division
Training Manager or Specialist	Kami	Charlene
Manager	Helene	Jim
Staff/Trainees	Eight technicians, including Frank	Twelve home nursing supervisors, including Elky 75 home health nurses and aides
Program One: Meeting Customer Needs Through Quality	One session Four technicians including Frank	Two sessions of the same workshop 75 staff members, in two groups
Program Two: Making Our Meetings More Productive	Four sessions, during staff meetings Helene's entire staff	Four sessions with other hospital staff attending Twelve home nursing supervisors

CHAPTER FOUR

DEVELOPING TRAINING FOR STRONG FOLLOW-THROUGH

A runner approaches the finish line. Fifty yards, then twenty, ten, five—then, a dead stop at the ribbon. Almost impossible—no running coach would allow one of his runners to do this. The running coach insists that his runners see beyond the line and move at top speed *through* the ribbon. Likewise, tennis and golf pros preach, *"Follow-through with that swing!"*

Less experienced managers and training staffs see completing the training materials and delivering the workshops or courses as the finish line. It's easy to see how this happens. Preparing the workbooks, renting the videos, producing the overheads, and making room arrangements focuses everyone's attention on tangible activities that can be seen, touched, counted, and scheduled.

Developing training programs is a systematic process. In general, the development process goes through thee interdependent phases outlined in the High-IMPACT Training™ Model.

HIGH-IMPACT TRAINING™ MODEL

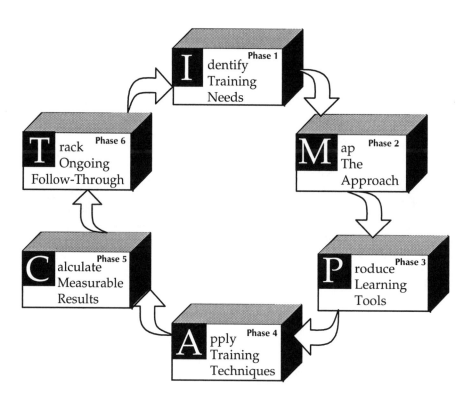

As in any system, each training phase depends on the previous ones, and impacts those that follow. A poor result in one phase will negatively affect the results of the next phase.

For many, follow-through is an afterthought—a vague task beyond the finish line. But the experienced manager and training staff understand that this is not the case. They see past the finish line and know that the end of the training program is precisely the time to continue running at top speed.

The first five phases of this training model are beyond the scope of this guidebook. This guidebook focuses on the last phase: Track Ongoing Follow-Through. However, this chapter does look at the complete High-IMPACT training model to identify the activities that need to happen in each of the phases to ensure strong training follow-through.

Phase One: Identify Training Needs

During Phase One, training developers committed to lasting training results will:

√ Recommend training for the right reasons. Good training is developed and delivered to improve skills or introduce new ones, not because the topic sounds interesting or because an organization has always done training on a particular subject.

√ Determine what skills are needed. Ask the learners. Ask the people who depend on the work the learners perform. Learn about the background, education, experience, and work environment of the learners. What kinds of problems do they try to solve?

√ Ask these questions: How do people feel about participating in the training program? Do they value the topics that are planned? How confident about learning are they? Do their supervisors value the training?

The knowledge that managers or training specialists gain by asking these kinds of questions is essential to the other phases. It sets the direction for the entire project. Without determining the real needs for new skills or behaviors, and then matching the training program to those needs, even the most comprehensive post-training effort will produce few results.

Phase Two: Map The Approach

The training development process is highly creative as well as systematic, and the approaches to adopt are unlimited. A good understanding of the learners' needs and supervisor's expectations provides the training professional a sense of direction. The combination of the basic elements of presentation, discussion, practice, and feedback, along with media choices, produces a program that meets the learners' needs and the practical considerations of time, budget, and resources.

During Phase Two, developers committed to training follow-through usually take these steps:

√ Consult representatives of the trainee group for their opinions on the training approach before it is finalized. Consider the views of others affected by the training: owners, supervisors, customers, and coworkers.

√ Prepare training objectives that describe the new behaviors, and suggest ways to measure the changes. Measures developed now guide managers and trainees as they prepare for the actual training and for training follow-through.

√ Select a training approach that respects and motivates the learners. A program delivered to adults needs to account for their prior experiences and build upon them. Adult learners can share a great deal with one another during the training, and can provide mutual support and feedback following the session.

√ All through the process, acknowledge that the real learning *(and testing of the learning)* takes place on the shop floor, in the purchasing department, or face-to-face with customers. Set reasonable expectations to achieve certain skill levels during the training; set higher expectations for the period following the training or with continuous practice opportunities.

√ Design the training with time and space for practice. Avoid the strong temptation to deliver more information than can be absorbed in the allotted time. Unless the trainees are traveling a long distance, plan to deliver the training in digestible segments. Include practice and feedback in each segment. Build confidence to carry the trainee through the variety of challenges he is likely to experience as he applies what he has learned.

Phase Three: Produce The Learning Tools

Learning tools are produced internally or externally by:

1. Internal trainers or training specialists. Sometimes managers are expected to create their own training tools.

2. External *(outside)* consultants or vendors contracted to work with the organization's training personnel or managers. This might include outside resources such as educational publishers, video producers, or software developers.

In Phase Three, each group must take steps to increase successful follow-through.

Internal training specialist

√ Check: Are the activities and exercises planned based in reality? Sometimes, training specialists are not familiar with the specific environments in which the trainees spend their days. For example, accompany a nurse on a home health visit. Or, watch a technician repair a circuit board and listen to her talk with customers on the telephone.

√ Coordinate and reinforce the terminology and content presented in one program with ideas or concepts presented in another. Watch for consistency in the training messages communicated in various programs.

√ Carefully plan small group activities. The correct size and composition of groups is important. For most topics, direct trainees to work with others from their own work groups. This increases the likelihood that ideas and plans will be implemented. The trainees become a maintenance or support system for one another after the training.

√ Produce materials that support not only the training session, but ongoing practices and projects. Use activities and materials that help the trainee set goals for implementation. Develop action plans that address probable barriers to use of the new skills.

For example, design worksheets and action plans that guide trainees into their learning future with questions such as:

○ What are the next three steps you want to take?
○ Which idea presented in today's session will you implement immediately?
○ What has to change for you to do something about the situation you described in the XYZ activity?
○ What do you need from your manager to help you apply the information from this program?

Outside consultants or vendors

The preceding considerations for the internal development of training materials also apply to consultants and vendors. If vendors are unable to customize their programs or meet these requirements within your budget, develop a plan to supplement the training yourself.

√ Check: Is the content included in the consultant's program relevant to a variety of on-the-job situations the trainees experience? Will the trainees recognize themselves and their organization in the material, in the videos, the case studies, etc.? If the examples do not look and feel familiar, learning is blocked.

√ Check: To what extent is the vendor ready and eager to customize a program to the organization's culture, industry context, and learning needs?

√ Check: How does the vendor's plan or product provide for follow-through? What kinds of support is the vendor prepared to offer managers and trainees after the program, and at what cost?

Usually, vendors do not plan for direct involvement in post-program activities because of the intermittent nature of follow-through tasks. Have the vendor provide a list of possible assignments, suggestions, or challenges that others can implement. Ask the vendor to assist managers with brief telephone consultations. Truly professional consultants want their packages and programs to bring results for their clients.

Phase Four: Apply Training Techniques

The best materials and the most creative exercises cannot compensate for a poorly presented training program. An effective trainer utilizes training techniques to facilitate learning.

√ Check: Does the person delivering the program have credibility with the trainee group? How can you establish this credibility? Does the instructor have enough personal experience with the content needed to role model skills and demonstrate their value? Personal experience and applications enliven the content, and inspire trainees to apply the concepts later.

√ Check: Will the instructor's presentation style make the learners comfortable? Does the trainer have the interpersonal skills it takes to manage a classroom of diverse personalities and needs?

√ Check: Does the facilitator believe in follow-through, and will she encourage the trainees to set firm goals? Will she coach on the skills over the next few months?

Phase Five: Calculate Measurable Results

You begin calculating measurable training results by asking, *"Are the trainees using the new skills?"* (or new procedures, information, etc.) or *"What difference did the training make?"* Calculating measurable results and tracking ongoing follow-through are closely related.

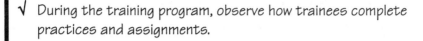
√ During the training program, observe how trainees complete practices and assignments.

√ Obtain evaluation data immediately following the training session. Ask for, and look closely at, feedback that identifies needs for follow-through (*e.g., more content or practice, more coaching, and more removal of barriers*).

√ Go beyond using a short feedback form at the end of the session. Conduct a more in-depth evaluation process to assess changes and improvements at two weeks, one month, three months, or whatever intervals are appropriate for the skills and information presented.

Phase Six: Track Ongoing Follow-Through

Individuals who are consulted or involved in any of the development phases must commit to successful follow-through. Unless they do, their efforts and talents produce little benefit. This phase is the focus of this guidebook.

√ In Chapter Five, you'll see what managers, training staff and trainees' do to prepare for follow-through before the training begins.

√ Chapter Six covers follow-through techniques to build into the training program.

√ Roles, responsibilities, special situations and creative training tools are covered in Chapters Seven, Eight, and Nine.

Summary

Individuals who are consulted or involved in any of the development phases must commit to successful follow-through. Unless they do, their efforts and talents produce little benefit.

CHAPTER FOUR WORKSHEET:
APPLYING A SYSTEMATIC APPROACH

1. Think about a current training project, preferably one that is just beginning or in the discussion stage. Briefly describe it here:

_____

_____

_____

_____

_____

_____

_____

_____

_____

_____

_____

_____

_____

_____

_____

_____

2. Next, for each of the first four development phases, identify one thing you can do to ensure that the trainees will not stop at the finish line.

a. Identify Training Needs

_____

_____

_____

b. Map The Approach

_____

_____

_____

c. Produce Learning Tools

_____

_____

_____

d. Apply Training Techniques

_____

_____

_____

CHAPTER FIVE

PREPARING FOR FOLLOW-THROUGH

As you develop or select the course, lay the groundwork for effective follow-through.

If you as the manager have initiated the training program, you are already committed to the preparation process. If others outside your department or work group have recommended or required the training program, you will need to request information about the design of the program to prepare for follow-through. Either way, your resources *(in people and time)* are expended in the training effort.

A few simple preparations on your part, and that of the training staff and the trainees, will ensure the lasting results that follow-through brings.

The Manager's Role In Preparation

Decide or clarify how the training event will benefit his/her people, improve their performance, and support the department's objectives.

Review the training objectives, and visualize in detail how to apply the new skills and ideas.

At first, Helene isn't thrilled at the prospect of sending anyone from her group to a half-day customer service workshop during the same week a major customer order is due.

Then, just after receiving the workshop announcement with the note from Kami *(Arrow's training specialist)*, strongly *encouraging* her group to participate, Helene overhears a telephone conversation between one of the technicians and a customer. The way the customer was treated in the conversation makes her wince. She decides that her investment of staff time—and some planning time on her part—will be worth it. She schedules four people from her eight-person staff to attend, and asks them to present a summary of key concepts and applications at the first staff meeting following the workshop.

 Communicate expectations and goals for the training. Seek staff needs and interests.

Compare the course objectives with the manager's goals for follow-through and the trainees' needs, interests, and expectations. A good match between planned topics, the manager's objectives, and the participants' needs and interests ensures motivated managers and learners.

Both Helene at Arrow Computer and Jim at Mountain Health realize that unproductive meetings waste everyone's time. They find though, that unless they personally plan and lead most of their meetings, the meetings often lose focus. Both are therefore committed to taking full advantage of this training opportunity.

Jim, at Mountain Health, has a strong desire to build his nursing supervisors' business skills and confidence. He must build them, because the demands on his own time are increasing by the day. Helene, at Arrow, sometimes feels that she has little in the way of technical expertise to contribute to many of the meetings, and would rather spend her time more productively elsewhere. Wisely, Helene and Jim also understand that before they can delegate more of the responsibility for running meetings, their staffs need training.

With their respective staffs, Helene and Jim review their own objectives. They preview the course outline and poll their people to get a sense of their interests and motivations.

December 10, 199X

NOTICE TO NURSING SUPERVISORS

Course Announcement:
Making Our Meetings More Productive

Presented by: Charlene, Human Resources Department

This course consists of four, two-hour sessions presented on alternate weeks, beginning the week of January 16. The course is designed to improve our skills in meeting preparation and management. Together, we can implement the ideas we learn.

Please review the session topics and objectives posted next to this announcement and indicate the following:

1. Your preference for session times (*either Tuesdays from 10 A.M. to 12 P.M., or Wednesdays from 1 P.M. to 3 P.M.*).

2. Any additional topics or issues you want addressed in the course as it relates to your nursing supervisor role or other professional needs.

3. At least one specific application you foresee for the skills you will learn.

Thanks, Jim.

Return your responses to the Human Resources Department by December 17, 199X.

Jim learns that one of his supervisors, Elky, is interested in taking classes in business administration at the local community college. Jim will now consider ways of involving Elky more heavily in the training follow-through activities.

Plan for follow-through practice and feedback activities to reinforce new or changed behaviors.

Practice and feedback need to begin immediately following the training, so managers prepare for this in advance. One of the best ways to reinforce the application of new skills or procedures is to consider them in goal setting and performance reviews that follow the training.

Jim consults with Elky in more detail and asks her to meet with Charlene to plan a number of post-training activities. For example, after the training and some practice time, Elky will arrange to have Charlene or another trainer observe a supervisors' meeting and provide feedback to the group. Jim and Elky also feel that adding a performance standard for *"meeting leadership"* to her job description is appropriate.

To measure both Elky's performance and the general productivity of the meetings, the supervisors will create a short meeting evaluation form based on a five-point scale. Every quarter, the supervisors will review the evaluation forms and note needed improvements.

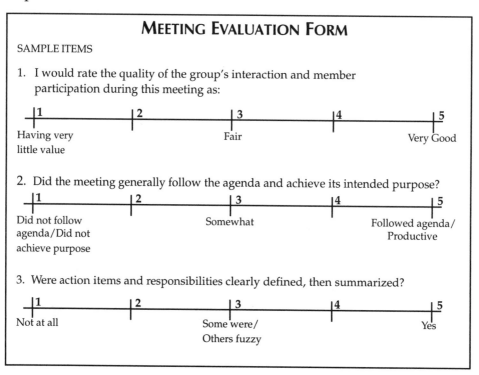

MEETING EVALUATION FORM

SAMPLE ITEMS

1. I would rate the quality of the group's interaction and member participation during this meeting as:

1	2	3	4	5
Having very little value		Fair		Very Good

2. Did the meeting generally follow the agenda and achieve its intended purpose?

1	2	3	4	5
Did not follow agenda/Did not achieve purpose		Somewhat		Followed agenda/ Productive

3. Were action items and responsibilities clearly defined, then summarized?

1	2	3	4	5
Not at all		Some were/ Others fuzzy		Yes

Jim and Elky also feel they agree on the following performance standard *(performance expectation)* to include in Elky's job description:

> *Functions as a meeting leader in a way that encourages effective group participation and achieves meeting objectives.*

Results from the completed meeting evaluation forms will also provide peer input on Elky's performance reviews.

At Arrow Computer, Helene is thinking ahead as well. She is a little concerned about the upcoming customer service training. How will she reinforce the information presented, then later measure improvements in customer service that result from the training or from staff discussions?

Helene asks Kami to contact Mario to inquire if his organization has prepared some kind of post-workshop checklist or measurement tool for managers to use. She receives a general checklist from Mario, but decides to modify this tool for her own purposes.

Helene wants to reinforce communication habits that the workshop is likely to encourage. She develops the following draft form for her technicians to use for two to three weeks following the training. Before finalizing the form, she will consult with Frank and the other workshop attendees for their suggestions.

POST-WORKSHOP CUSTOMER SERVICE CHECKLIST

Complete for a minimum of five calls per day.

❏ Date: _____

❏ Customer: _____

❏ Primary Phone or Fax Number: _____

❏ Best Time of Day to Reach: _____

❏ Alternative Phone Number: _____

❏ Briefly describe the nature of the call or visit:

❏ What were this customer's main concerns?

❏ Example of one clarifying question you used during the inter-action:

❏ Example of one open-ended question you used during the interaction:

❏ I confirmed the delivery date.   Yes No

❏ I referred to the customer by name at least twice during the interaction.   Yes No

❏ I thanked the customer for his or her business, or otherwise indicated that we were glad to be of service.   Yes No

Provide input to the training design, as requested. Offer ideas for follow-through.

When managers take the time to review course descriptions and objectives, there are fewer surprises during and after the training. Managers are responsible for finding out about the content of training programs their employees attend. Sometimes, there are opportunities for managers to participate in the program design or review the course in detail prior to its delivery.

Managers can assist training specialists with suggestions related to:

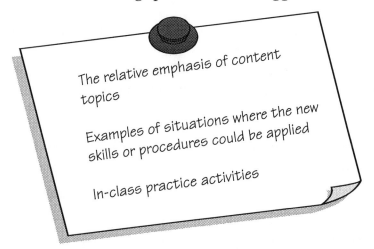

The relative emphasis of content topics

Examples of situations where the new skills or procedures could be applied

In-class practice activities

Kami understands the time pressures on Helene's group. The meeting effectiveness course was scheduled to begin just two weeks after the customer service training was added to the schedule. Kami asks Helene for her thoughts about scheduling. Helene responds with a rather unique plan for her group— combining the training with regularly scheduled, biweekly staff meetings.

Kami decides that a similar format might work well for other departments. She sees the added benefit of trainees immediately applying meeting principles and procedures introduced in the course. After the first training session, the technicians' own staff meetings would serve as practice opportunities.

In this case, Helene's input served not only her own group's needs, but benefited the entire organization.

The Training Staff's Role In Preparation

 Follow good training development practices.

As the training staff develops and reviews materials, activities and exercises, they need to consider the desired outcomes of each activity. How will trainees follow-through on them? If the trainees were to ask, *"What's next?"* or *"What do I do with this on Monday morning"*—would the answers be clear? Does each activity in the training apply to something the trainees need to do, say, or feel back on the job?

It is the training staff's responsibility to take these questions into account. Following the phases of the training development cycle outlined in Chapter Four will produce good training experiences and help trainees transfer *(or carry over)* the learning to real work applications.

View the trainees' manager as an important internal customer and critical to the success of the follow-through.

Check out the manager's needs.

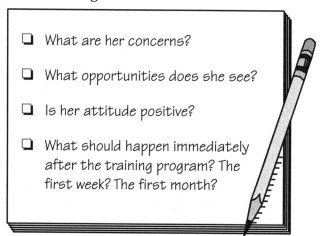

❑ What are her concerns?

❑ What opportunities does she see?

❑ Is her attitude positive?

❑ What should happen immediately after the training program? The first week? The first month?

One of the training specialist's roles is to coach and motivate the manager in advance of the training. If the manager is neutral toward the training effort, the chance for skills and changes to take firm root is limited.

Jim expresses his concerns about the customer service workshop to Charlene. Jim wants a clear return on his investment of 300 staff hours *(75 people x 4 hours/person)* spent attending the workshop. Jim views his home health customer population as unique, and is uncertain about the value of a generic program.

Charlene understands, and helps Jim anticipate useful follow-through activities. She makes suggestions on how to incorporate the concepts presented in the workshops into the division's next series of customer interviews. She also knows that one unit in the workshop demonstrates the process of creating a customer service improvement plan. Charlene explains to Jim that the results from the survey his department plans to conduct will provide excellent input to the kind of improvement plan recommended in the course. *(In the Appendix, a blank version of this form is available to copy and use.)*

ACTIVITY ANALYSIS FOR TRAINING SPECIALISTS

Training Program: Meeting Customer Needs Through Quality
Presented By: Mario
Developer/Writer: Mario
Presentation Date: November 15, 199X

1. Training activity, event or unit—and time spent in this activity:

   Asking for Customer Feedback *(two sessions).*

2. Outcome of activity *(what is produced, learned, etc.)*:

   Ideas about ways to ask for customer feedback. Ideas about the variety of formal and informal tools that can be used.

3. How, when, or under what conditions will the skill or information developed in this activity be applied on the job?

   Jim's supervisors are planning their next series of in-depth customer interviews. This is a major component of their local market research.

4. Ideas for on-the-job practice or application activities:

   Develop tools to use with various types of customers, families, and physicians.

5. Feedback on practice or application: What should the manager or training specialist observe in the practice?

   Review draft tools for clarity. Encourage a pilot test.

6. Additional resources to build skills or improve practice:

   Assistance with drafting questions.

The Trainee's Role In Preparation

Know the purpose for the training and identify follow-through activities.

At the technicians' weekly staff meeting, Helene offers a few specific examples of customer service issues. *"We could use some improvement,"* she begins. She reviews the topics of the customer service training, and conveys her plan for having four members of the group summarize and share key concepts and ideas with the others.

> *"Frank, how would you feel about attending the workshop and taking responsibility for leading the review session with us?"* asks Helene. *"We'll rely on you and the others to select the ideas and materials from the presentation that we really need."*

Although he might not admit it, Frank is more energized now that he has a clear purpose for attending. Frank plans to identify the key concepts from the training that will need to be practiced in the first three weeks back on the job.

Request and review the training agenda. Complete the requested prework.

Some of the home health nurses are having the same concerns that Frank expressed. They feel their level of customer service is already quite good. One week before Mario's program is delivered at Mountain Health, a two-page article on *Moments of Truth* appears in each of their office mailboxes, with instructions to please read the article in advance of the workshop.

Regina, a highly qualified and experienced nurse who is not particularly excited about the idea of nonclinical training, is intrigued with the article's title and first paragraph. She turns two pages ahead to see an outline of the workshop. Her mind opens to the possibility that the workshop might include a few good points.

CHECKLIST OF PREPARATION STEPS

For managers...

1. Decide or clarify how the training will benefit your people, improve their performance, and support the department's objectives.

2. Communicate expectations and goals for the training session. Seek staff needs and interests.

3. Plan time for follow-through practice and feedback activities to reinforce new or changed behaviors.

4. Provide input to the training design, as requested. Offer ideas for follow-through.

For training staff...

1. Follow good training development practices.

2. View the trainees' manager as an important internal customer who is critical to the success of the follow-through.

For trainees...

1. Know the purpose for the training and identify several personal benefits.

2. Request and review the training agenda. Complete the requested prework.

Summary

Effective training and successful follow-through require creative thinking and careful planning on the part of the manager, the training staff, and the trainee. You can anticipate many needs for training follow-through, such as setting up relevant practice opportunities, removing barriers that block people from applying new skills, coaching, etc. If you anticipate these needs, you can address them in the design of the program, in preparation, and in scheduling. The earlier you address needs for follow-through, the better your chance for success.

Chapter Six visits our groups as they experience their workshops and sessions. Through a series of snapshots, you'll see how the preparation begins to pay off.

CHAPTER FIVE WORKSHEET:
PREPARE TO FOLLOW-THROUGH

1. Recall a recent training experience that members of your staff
    attended. What were two things you did to prepare yourself
    and your staff for the training?

    _____

    _____

    _____

    _____

    _____

2. Knowing the results of the training, what else would you have
    done to prepare, given the same opportunity?

    _____

    _____

    _____

    _____

    _____

    _____

3. Consider an upcoming or potential training program. List three things you can do with your staff to ensure successful follow-through.

_____

_____

_____

_____

_____

_____

_____

TRAINING SNAPSHOTS

We now join our four training groups in progress. First, we'll look into the training rooms as Arrow's technicians and Mountain Health's nursing staff experience the *Meeting Customer Needs Through Quality* workshop.

Next, we sit in as the technicians and nursing supervisors participate in *Making Our Meetings More Productive*.

Workshop Agenda

Workshop Title:
Meeting Customer Needs Through Quality

Group Discussion: Great And Not So Great Customer Service

Small Group Activity: Our Customers' Perceptions And Expectations

Presentation: Moments Of Truth Video Presentation

Presentation/Discussion: Relationships With Internal And External Customers

Presentation/Demonstration: Asking For Customer Feedback

Presentation/Demonstration: Skills For Listening To Customers

Summary Presentation: What It Takes To Provide Quality Customer Service

- Technical Competence
- Systems Support
- Interpersonal Skills

Presentation and Small Group Activity: The Customer Service Improvement Plan

Arrow Technicians' Customer Service Training

Four technicians have left piles of work at their stations to attend this session. They have agreed to prepare a summary of key points for presentation at their next staff meeting.

TIME: 8:25 A.M.

EVENT: Group activity—Customer perceptions and expectations

The technicians choose to collaborate for this 20-minute activity to identify their customers' service expectations. They use a workbook page that contains key points and questions for taking notes. Because they work together daily and deal with the same customers, they are able to focus their discussion and ideas on specific customer situations.

A follow-through opportunity:

The Arrow technicians have—for these 20 minutes—become a customer service troubleshooting team. In some ways, this activity was a team-building exercise. Together they have examined and diagnosed potential sources for customer service problems. They will continue to build their frame of reference during group activities later in the workshop, and back in their department.

TIME: 8:55 A.M.

EVENT: The customer service video and debrief

Mario takes a few minutes after the video presentation to solicit comments from the group. He asks, *"What do these scenes suggest about your customers' needs?"* Mario's brief review of a just-completed activity *(sometimes called a debrief)* helps the trainees put new ideas into focus and relate important customer service concepts to one another.

How these events support training follow-through:

The images of customer service presented in the video are easily recalled because they are true-to-life and visual, and therefore more engaging and memorable than verbal explanations. Trainees who view good videos are likely to remember key messages. The situations depicted in the customer service video are close enough to the technicians' world that they can apply the key points to their own situations.

TIME: 11:05 A.M.
EVENT: Group activity—preparing the customer service improvement plan

 Using a planning procedure included in the workbook, the technicians discuss the steps required to address their department's customer service issues.

One of the steps asks them to list possible barriers to providing good service, and prioritize them as *"Most significant," "Second most significant,"* etc. Mario suggests that they use their group work as a starting point for creating a Customer Service Improvement Plan.

How these activities support training follow-through:

Discussing barriers in a training session encourages trainees to think in specific ways about what needs to happen after the training. Often, questions about barriers are followed by questions related to overcoming the barriers and developing action lists.

Through this activity, combined with the earlier discussion of perceptions and expectations, the technicians have built a foundation for future discussion and action planning. They are on their way to creating the Improvement Plan.

Mario And The Home Health Care Division
(Afternoon Session)

TIME: 1:55 P.M.

EVENT: The customer service video presentation

Unlike the Arrow technicians, the nursing trainees have difficulty relating any of the characters or situations to their work. None of the examples depicted in the video relate to health care or the unusual circumstances of the nurses' customers—recently discharged hospital patients.

A follow-through opportunity is lost:

Many of the potential benefits of this training tool are lost because the video did not come close enough to matching the trainees' work environment or customers.

TIME: 4:50 P.M.

EVENT: Post-program assignment

Mario issues a challenge to the workshop participants: Keep a log of the Moments of Truth *(examples of excellent customer service)* and Moments of Misery *(examples of poor customer service)* they experience for two weeks. For each moment logged, the nurses are also asked to briefly describe how good listening skills contributed to the moment of truth, or how a failure to listen contributed to a moment of misery. Trainees are asked to discuss the assignment with their supervisors after two weeks.

A possible, but not guaranteed, follow-through opportunity:

The post-program assignment ties together two of the important concepts taught in the workshops: That very good and very poor customer service takes place in brief moments—and that listening skills are critical to good customer service. Because the assignment is short, relevant, and sounds interesting, trainees are more likely to complete it.

However, *Meeting Customer Needs Through Quality* is a one-session training program. The benefits of training follow-through will depend, in part, on whether or not a training specialist or the trainees' manager checks back on the assignment.

Arrow Technicians' Training Session On Meetings

Helene and Kami have worked out a unique plan for the *Making Our Meetings More Productive* training session for the technicians. Because the technicians' time pressures are intense, Helene and Kami decide to deliver the four sessions during actual staff meetings, held biweekly on Tuesday mornings. Today is Session Three. The topic is Basics of Group Dynamics.

COURSE OUTLINE

Course Title: *Making Our Meetings More Productive*

Session One: Planning The Meeting
Meeting Purposes
Meeting Roles
Logistics And Details That Make Meetings Work

Session Two: Developing And Using The Meeting Agenda
Discussion: Assignment From Session One
Meeting Roles
Strategies For Constructing The Meeting

Session Three: Basics Of Group Dynamics
Verbal And Nonverbal Communication
Listening And Speaking In Meetings
Levels Of Contributing In Meetings
Discussion: Assignment From Session Two
Setting And Using Meeting Ground Rules

Session Four: Meeting Facilitation
Discussion: Assignment From Session Three
Review: The Facilitator's Role
Using The Group Memory
Consensus Building
Meeting Follow-Up

TIME: 7:30 A.M.

EVENT: Presentation on verbal and nonverbal
communication

As Kami presents the topic of nonverbal
communication during meetings, two of the
technicians comment that somewhat different
guidelines on the same topic were presented during the previous
Meeting Customer Needs Through Quality workshop. A short
discussion to clarify the concepts follows.

How this activity supports training follow-through:

The agenda for the training session must allow time and flexibility
for questions and clarifications. Kami handles them as they are
raised. If the technicians had left this session confused about
interpreting nonverbal messages, they might have dismissed the
key points altogether—before trying to apply them. Follow-
through and application would not be possible.

TIME: 8:05 A.M.

EVENT: Small project assignment; review of
previous assignment

The technicians are reviewing and discussing their
observation logs from a project assigned in Session Two.
The assignment required the participants to observe 15-
to 30-minute portions of two meetings in which they did not play a
major role.

An observation log was provided to record their observations
about the participants' roles *(e.g., who was contributing, how often, in
what manner, etc.)* and how the meeting participants' contributions
affected the progress of the meeting.

Follow-through opportunity:

When a training program is divided into multiple sessions, there are opportunities between sessions for application and practice. Short projects with clear instructions are assigned. Then, at the next session, the instructor spends time debriefing, or reviewing the practice project. In this case, questions such as, *"What did you observe about how people performed their roles?"* and *"How do you think assigning roles helped the outcome of the meeting?"* are good review questions.

The design of *Making Our Meetings More Productive* takes advantage of multiple sessions and the time between sessions. The technicians already attend several meetings each week; each meeting now provides an opportunity for practice. Practice projects are most effective if their purposes and instructions are specific. Others outside the training program, such as the trainees' manager or coworkers not attending the training, sometimes need to be aware that practice projects have been assigned.

- Short practice projects are assigned at each session. These are to be completed on the job by the following session or by the end of the program.

- Practice projects give participants a chance to work with concepts and skills introduced in the session.

- Problems encountered, questions, and results from the practices are discussed during the following session.

- The between-session practice projects supplement, rather than replace, short practices within the training session.

The following illustrates how practice assignments from *Making Our Meetings More Productive* are assigned, reviewed, and how they contribute to training follow-through, even before the course is completed.

Follow-Through Practice Opportunities In A Multiple-Session Design

Session One: Planning The Meeting

- Assign Practice Project # 1

Session Two: Developing And Using The Meeting Agenda

- Review and discuss Assignment # 1
- Assign Practice Projects # 2 and # 3

Session Three: Basics Of Group Dynamics

- Review and discuss Assignment # 2
- Discuss questions on Assignment # 3, due at Session Four
- Assign Practice Project # 4

Session Four: Meeting Facilitation

- Review and discuss Assignment # 4
- Trainee Reports or Presentations on Assignment # 3
- Discuss Follow-Through Assignments for Post-Training

Post-Training

- Feedback from training specialist or manager on follow-through activities assigned in Session Four

TIME: 8:25 A.M.

EVENT: Setting and using meeting ground rules

Kami leads a group brainstorming session on ground rules that will help the technicians' meetings. The group realizes that two sets of ground rules are needed: one for meetings within their own work group or involving other departments; another set for customer meetings. The group proceeds to develop two lists. Kami allows ten minutes at the end of the activity for them to select the most useful and practical ground rules from each list.

Ground Rules

How this activity supports training follow-through:

Work and plans for on-the-job implementation were accomplished in this short activity. The activity demonstrated and provided practice in running a productive meeting discussion. There was a clear goal, a process to reach the goal, involvement, and the ideas of many people coming together.

Not only do the participants leave today's session with a customized product that will enable them to hold more productive meetings, they have experienced firsthand what meeting productivity feels like.

⛰️ More Productive Meetings For Nursing Supervisors

Improved meeting skills are a priority for the supervisors who meet on a daily basis. At one time, Jim estimated that his supervisors spent 30 to 40 percent of their time in meetings. Jim and the supervisors are aware that communication and coordination keep their division working.

TIME: 1:15 P.M.

EVENT: Session one—meeting types and meeting roles

 The supervisors are working in pairs to define and describe the types of meetings they typically plan and attend, and the meeting roles of the attendees (*leader, facilitator, recorder, timekeeper, etc.*). The instructor for the course has presented a list of general meeting types and roles. Now the trainees are working in small groups, translating these generic lists into a more specific planning sheet to use for their own meetings.

How this activity supports training follow-through:

The small group discussion is a practice activity in identifying meeting types and roles. Because the nursing supervisors have a chance to immediately apply the information presented, they are more likely to remember and use it after the course.

This chapter has presented numerous examples of training room events and tools that have the potential to motivate and guide follow-through activities. You can adapt the training activities discussed in this chapter to training on any topic.

Type Of Training Activity Checklist

Use this worksheet as you review a proposed training program to plan for training follow-through.

Type of training activity

Is this type of event or activity found in the planned program? If not, could it be added or could a planned activity be modified?

Ask: Is the activity used to its full potential for training follow-through?

Ask: How can I improve the activity?

❑ Videos that present situations and styles the participants relate to, and can recall and visualize later

❑ Activity debriefs *(reviews)* and discussions that help the trainees pull new ideas together, summarize what they have learned, and take the ideas away from the course

❑ Small-group activities that allow trainees from the same work unit to plan for strong follow-through tasks

❑ Training materials that summarize key content and prompt trainees to plan for actions they will need to take post-training

❑ (If the program is more than several hours) Multiple sessions that offer a progressive series of projects or assignments to be accomplished between sessions

❑ Time for practice activities within the training session

❑ Time for clarification and discussion during the program

❑ Instructor modeling of new behaviors

❑ Post-program assignments and goal setting

CHAPTER SIX WORKSHEET: BUILDING FOLLOW-THROUGH INTO YOUR TRAINING

1. Review the design of a planned or current training program. Briefly describe this program.

_____

_____

_____

_____

_____

_____

_____

_____

_____

_____

_____

_____

_____

_____

_____

2. Use the checklist on page 59 to identify the kinds of activities
and events that will contribute to training follow-through in
this program. The design of your training program might have
included other follow-through opportunities—note these as
well.

_____

_____

_____

_____

_____

_____

_____

_____

_____

_____

_____

_____

_____

_____

_____

_____

_____

AFTER THE TRAINING

It's over. The evaluation forms are collected. Everyone has left the training room. The paper charts are rolled up and labeled, and one last soft drink remains on the refreshment table. People seemed reasonably pleased and upbeat when they left. Was the program successful? Perhaps. Actually, the changes in skills, behavior, and attitude begin now. And if you are the trainees' manager, your job begins now as well. It's time for implementing training follow-through.

The Manager's Responsibilities

 Provide an application assignment immediately following the program.

As the series of four meeting effectiveness sessions progresses, Jim of Mountain Health is excited about the possibilities of his having to attend fewer meetings. The morning after the fourth session, Jim arranges a meeting with Elky to hear her overall impressions of the training and to plan practice assignments.

Together, they quickly develop a list of meetings that one or more supervisors from the Home Health Care Division are expected to attend elsewhere in the hospital. The meetings are included on the division's own agenda. They agree to adapt *(with revisions)* one of the observation logs used in the training program. They will distribute logs to the supervisors with instructions to complete one for every meeting they attend for a period of three weeks. Then they will discuss and summarize the results. Finally, the managers will develop improvement strategies.

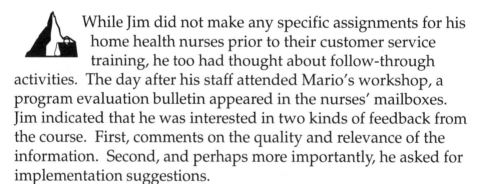

"Oh, and by the way Elky, will you arrange your schedule to plan and facilitate the next monthly supervisors' meeting?" asked Jim. "Let me take a quick look at the agenda you prepare a few days ahead of time so that we can finalize it. I'll be at the meeting, but I want you to run it. You and I can meet for 15 minutes or so afterwards to review how you did."

Jim asks Elky, in the meantime, to contact a number of the other supervisors to get their feedback on *Making Our Meetings More Productive*. Jim wants to hear any comments the supervisors did not take the time to include on the short evaluation forms distributed at the end of the session. He will forward the comments to Charlene, so that the training department has the benefit of more detailed feedback.

 Communicate the follow-through plan. Monitor and measure progress.

 At Arrow Computer, Helene laid the groundwork for good follow-through when she suggested that Frank take responsibility for reporting to the group after the workshop.

 While Jim did not make any specific assignments for his home health nurses prior to their customer service training, he too had thought about follow-through activities. The day after his staff attended Mario's workshop, a program evaluation bulletin appeared in the nurses' mailboxes. Jim indicated that he was interested in two kinds of feedback from the course. First, comments on the quality and relevance of the information. Second, and perhaps more importantly, he asked for implementation suggestions.

Implement action plans to reduce workplace barriers that make it difficult to adopt newly learned behaviors.

Managers must revise established practices and procedures that conflict with new methods introduced in the training. If managers' expectations for employee performance do not change to match the new skills, the new skills will not be applied.

One notion that struck Frank and his fellow trainees during the *Meeting Customer Needs Through Quality* workshop was the idea that customer perceptions of the technicians' role and expertise did not match their own. Julie, one of the other technicians, commented during their training group activity that customers sometimes talked to her over the telephone as if she were repairing a toaster. They just didn't understand what was involved and didn't seem to acknowledge the level of expertise required to do their work.

Customers' Perception   **Technicians' Perception**

At the first staff meeting following the training program, Julie's point was brought up as a part of Frank's summary. To Helene's surprise, everyone reported having similar reactions. An immediate, short-term objective was set: convey a more professional image in telephone and face-to-face dealings with Arrow Computer's customers. A brainstorming session followed, then a discussion of ways to track and measure improvements. Key ideas from the workshop were translated into action plan steps and guidelines.

However, Helene knew that in trying to apply all the ideas from the workshop at once, the group would lose their focus and interest. Helene also knew that if the group's work on one goal—this first application from the training course—was successful, confidence and faith in the process would result.

Several months later, following their *Making Our Meetings More Productive* series, Charlene at Mountain Health and Kami at Arrow experienced the bonus of having key ideas from the two training programs connect. Working out the details of the ongoing customer service action plan became a way for the technicians to practice newly learned meeting and facilitation skills.

4. Reinforce improved performance and change.

Meetings became an important part of Elky's day-to-day responsibilities—planning them, running them, and following-through on action items developed during them. Two months after the training, Jim noticed how often he relied on Elky for the meeting responsibilities he once handled. Along with a favorable performance rating, Jim asked Mountain Health's Human Resources office to analyze and redefine Elky's job duties. The result was a new title and a higher pay grade.

New Title

Helene was able to use Frank's work on the customer issues as the basis for a good performance rating in the area of teamwork. Actually, Helene noticed an improvement in many of her staff member's teamwork ratings. Helene felt so positive that she considered incorporating peer review as one component of the next performance review.

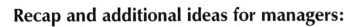

Recap and additional ideas for managers:

1. **Provide an application assignment immediately following the program.**

   ❏ Check in with trainees on any practice assignment issued during the training program.

   ❏ Observe and provide feedback.

   ❏ Plan next assignments and increase the challenge level.

   ❏ Provide feedback to training specialists involved in developing the program.

2. **Communicate the follow-through plan. Monitor and measure progress.**

   ❏ Clarify and modify procedures to accommodate new concepts.

   ❏ Translate between guidelines offered in the training and real-life conditions on the job.

   ❏ Measure the new performance against preset goals *(set prior to or during the training)*.

   ❏ Set higher goals as early goals are achieved.

3. **Implement an action plan to reduce workplace barriers that make it difficult to adopt newly learned behaviors.**

   ❏ Use lists or preliminary action plans generated during the training session.

   ❏ Establish which barriers the group can address within their own department. Make progress in this area first, then strategize on barriers that involve other work groups.

   ❏ Involve staff that did not attend the training program.

   ❏ Use continuous quality improvement tools the group knows.

4. **Reinforce improved performance and change.**

   ❏ Model the new behaviors yourself.

   ❏ Continue to apply performance measures.

   ❏ Deliver rewards.

   ❏ Formally acknowledge performance improvement and development in performance evaluations.

   ❏ Provide the trainees opportunities to coach and train others.

The Training Staff's Responsibilities

The training staff has the responsibility to support the manager's and trainees' follow-through efforts.

 Be available and offer support.

Motivate and encourage the manager to follow-through on the concepts and practices presented in the training program. Remind the manager of follow-through opportunities and prompt her with suggestions for coaching and encouraging the staff.

Check in with the manager periodically to see how the implementation of action plans, new skills, and other follow-through activities are progressing. Feedback from the manager provides valuable insights to the training staff, who are primarily concerned with how the training impacts their jobs.

Even though training and human resources personnel cannot work directly with every manager, they can offer support. For example, send messages and suggestions over the electronic mail system or quick notes by fax to distant offices. Staying in touch lets the managers know that you are available and thinking about their success.

 Assist with data collection.

Suggest ways for the managers to document performance improvements. Show the managers examples of how other departments keep track of their results.

Observation with checklists is one good method to use. The checklists can include the steps of a new procedure, behaviors demonstrated, or behaviors not demonstrated.

 At Mountain Health, Charlene assigns one of her training interns to observe the supervisors' meetings and complete a checklist of effective behaviors. Elky finds this feedback very helpful.

Following is a sample of the checklist.

MEETING FACILITATOR EVALUATION FORM

Meeting Date:_____

Meeting Facilitator:_____

Indicate the number of times the following facilitator behaviors and tasks were observed during this meeting. Add any comments.

1. Previewed the meeting/reviewed desired outcomes

2. Reviewed and made adjustments to the meeting agenda

3. Maintained focus on the agenda topic(s) as the meeting progressed

4. Managed time frames of agenda items

5. Helped the group reach and record its conclusions as the meeting progressed

6. Summarized conclusions/checked for agreement

7. Specified actions for meeting follow-through

8. Determined ways to monitor follow-through tasks.

Trainees can also record their own performance or results in terms of frequency *(how many times something happened)* or other measures.

Following the *Making Our Meetings More Productive* course at Arrow Computer, two of Helene's technicians keep a check sheet that, among other results, records the actual starting and ending times of meetings compared to the planned starting and ending times. Because late meeting starts and long meetings had been significant problems prior to the course, the group agreed this was important data to collect.

Check Sheet			
Meeting Times			
Planned Start	Actual Start	Planned End	Actual End
6/25 11:30	11:48	1:00	1:43
7/05 8:15	8:27	10:00	10:55
8/15 3:00	3:17	5:00	5:24
8/30 2:00	2:10	3:00	3:45

Whatever measures and methods are used to record changes, it is important to involve staff members in the design and use of the tools, and interpretation of the data collected with them.

Sometimes, organizations administer a pretest or pre-training assessment of trainee skills and knowledge. The training staff can support managers by assisting with the post-training test, interpreting the results, and giving feedback to the trainees.

3. Observe results, and recognize good efforts on everyone's part.

Kami and Charlene periodically check in with the managers. Kami, for instance, finds several amusing cartoons on customer service and sends them to Helene with a note to the technicians: *"Hear you're all doing great things. Next year we'll let you give the training program. Thanks!"*

At Mountain Health, Charlene knows that at least two dozen of the 75 nurses were not completely satisfied with Mario's course. This is because the video and other activities did not take into account the special nature of the patient-customer relationship. Charlene lets Jim know that she is researching training video catalogs to identify titles that are more focused on health care.

Kami at Arrow Computer and Charlene at Mountain Health know that Helene and Jim do a good job of coaching their staffs and believe in the process of training follow-through. Still, Helene and Jim appreciate reinforcement for their good efforts. Recognition motivates them and increases their commitment to follow-through.

4. Complete a thorough course evaluation.

The typical, brief course evaluation forms distributed to impatient trainees at the end of a workshop are only an initial, quick assessment of the trainees' satisfaction with the program. Rather than measuring results, this form of program evaluation usually establishes only whether or not the trainees liked the program. True course evaluation goes much further.

Kami is excited about comparing how two different formats for the *Making Our Meetings More Productive* program worked. Two weeks after their final session, she seeks feedback from Helene's technician group. She solicits similar feedback from another manager who, along with his staff members, attended the four sessions with staff and managers from many other departments.

Recap for training specialists:

1. Be available and offer support.

2. Assist with data collection.

3. Observe results, and recognize good efforts on everyone's part.

4. Complete a thorough course evaluation.

The Trainee's Responsibilities

The initial period of practicing new behaviors and applying new skills is often awkward and uncertain. Trainees are tempted to return to previous, more comfortable behaviors. If trainees are uncertain about how to apply new information in situations not directly addressed in the training, they will use old methods. Trainees must know that the training staff and their manager are willing to help them use what they have learned. Feedback and reinforcement from one's manager and more experienced peers is critical.

1. **Ask for feedback from your manager and peers.**
Trainees do not need to wait for feedback from others. They can initiate the process by communicating that feedback is needed and welcome. For example, ask:

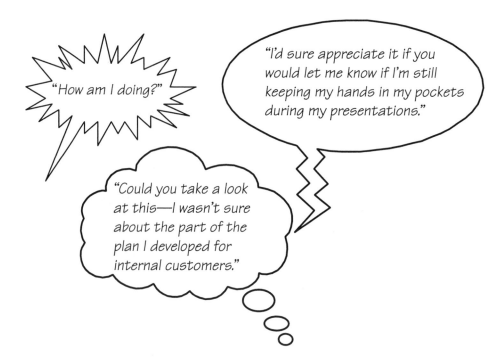

The faster the feedback is requested and given, and the more specific it is, the faster the trainee will demonstrate good results.

2. Communicate to training staff and managers about ongoing needs.

Several weeks after their *Meeting Customer Needs Through Quality* program, a nurses' committee assigned to revise the home health care division's customer survey tools is frustrated. They are having problems limiting the number of questions on their draft forms and writing the questions clearly. In several pilot tests of their survey, they find that many of the questions are misinterpreted. Their supervisor suggests they contact Charlene.

Charlene introduces them to a statistician who works in another hospital division. He offers to review their draft list and provide feedback and suggestions. Because the committee communicated their needs and sought expert help, the momentum of their effort wasn't seriously disrupted.

Recap for the trainee:

1. Ask for feedback from your manager and peers.

2. Communicate ongoing needs to training staff and your manager.

POST-TRAINING CHECKLIST	
GENERAL STEPS	**SPECIFIC STEPS**
For Managers... ❏ Provide an application assignment immediately following the program. ❏ Communicate the follow-through plan. Monitor and measure progress. ❏ Implement an action plan to reduce workplace barriers that make it difficult to adopt newly learned behaviors. ❏ Reinforce improved performance and change.	
For Training Staff... ❏ Be available and offer support. ❏ Assist with data collection. ❏ Observe results, and recognize good efforts on everyone's part. ❏ Complete a thorough course evaluation.	
For Trainees... ❏ Ask for feedback from your manager and peers. ❏ Communicate ongoing needs to training staff and your manager.	

Summary

In a working environment that values training and learning, the roles of the manager, training staff, and trainees overlap during the follow-through phase. Communication among managers, specialists, and staff takes the form of goal clarification, observation, feedback, and recognition.

CHAPTER SEVEN WORKSHEET:
BEYOND YOUR TRAINING SESSION

1. Think about the most recent training that you attended as a
trainee, or that members of your staff attended.

What was the subject?

_____

2. What were two key changes you planned to achieve after the
training program?

_____

_____

_____

_____

3. For each of the two changes, what behaviors are you looking
for and what observations do you hope to make?

_____

_____

_____

_____

_____

_____

4. Design a simple checklist or record-keeping tool to measure individual or group improvements on the skills or behaviors taught in the training program. Base the checklist on the behaviors and observations outlined in the previous question.

CHAPTER EIGHT

SPECIAL SITUATIONS

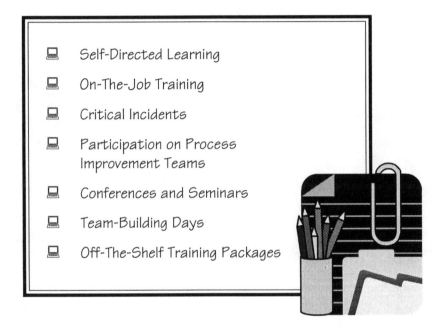

There are many ways of learning besides the traditional classroom or seminar setting. Each requires attention to follow-through. Examples of special learning opportunities include:

- 🖥 Self-Directed Learning

- 🖥 On-The-Job Training

- 🖥 Critical Incidents

- 🖥 Participation on Process Improvement Teams

- 🖥 Conferences and Seminars

- 🖥 Team-Building Days

- 🖥 Off-The-Shelf Training Packages

Self-Directed Learning

Many books, videotapes, audiotapes, books on tape, manuals, workbooks, and computer-aided instruction kits are available today. They cover thousands of topics ranging from accounting to teamwork. Designed for personal study, these individual resources are self-directed learning tools. Like traditional classroom training, self-directed learning also requires follow-through for best results.

The following ideas lay the groundwork for self-directed learning:

⊟   Know the benefits of the program. For example, is it for information, skill, or a new approach to negotiation?

⊟   Set personal goals by answering the question, "What do I want from this?"

⊟   Consider how you will measure your results. How will you know you have met your goal?

⊟   Plan and schedule your own practice time.

⊟   Enlist the help of others or ask others for feedback.

⊟   Decide on a reward for yourself.

Charlene pursued self-directed learning by purchasing an audiotape designed to help improve her business vocabulary. She listened to the tape 15 minutes a day for three weeks. Her goal was to use three new words every day in her writing or presentations. Charlene also asked a coworker to review her 15 new words every Friday over coffee.

On-The-Job Training

The goal of on-the-job training is to master a new skill, a new computer program, or a technique while you are using it. On-the-job training is not a casual process. Like a student pilot who must clock hours of flying practice with the instructor and then fly alone for hundreds of hours before earning a license, the trainee must have an organized program. A well-planned program includes a schedule that allows time for practice. The on-the-job trainee needs coaching from a manager, an instructor, or a qualified peer to build confidence in the new skills and provide feedback.

A useful tool for more effective on-the-job training follow-through is a daily journal in tape-recorded or written format. Questions such as the following are helpful. The answers can serve as discussion topics at scheduled coaching sessions.

♦ Where did I notice improvement today?

♦ Where am I unsure?

♦ What am I avoiding?

♦ What is my goal for tomorrow?

Critical Incidents

Critical incidents are important events. They include the announcement of a contract won or lost, the departure of a key person, a strong letter of complaint or praise, a crisis averted, or a challenge met.

Popular wisdom says that experience is the best teacher. Too often, organizations don't learn from their successes, mistakes, or experiences. Although employees talk about the experience or point fingers, most organizations stop short and fail to draw appropriate lessons. They don't ask, *"What does this incident teach us?"*

To truly learn from experience, it is necessary for individuals and groups to dig for these answers:

❑ How did we handle this situation?

❑ Did we use all the resources available?

❑ What should we have done differently?

❑ What did we do well?

❑ Has this happened before; is there a pattern or a trend?

❑ Do we need to change a policy or procedure? Take action?

❑ Do we need to communicate something?
   To whom?

Process Improvement Teams

As they complete assignments, task forces or quality teams build on their recent experiences by taking some time to become active learners and better team participants. Team experiences offer opportunities for learning if the members take time to examine the lessons gained from solving an urgent problem or improving a process.

Team members can discuss questions like the following and take action based on the responses.

☞ Did we meet our goal and to what business objective did our work contribute?

☞ Did we use all the resources available?

☞ What would we have done differently?

☞ What did we do well?

☞ Do we need to change or modify one of our own processes? Take action?

☞ Do we need to communicate something and to whom?

☞ What are our five best lessons learned?

☞ How shall we reward or celebrate our success?

The team that follows-through summarizes their best methods and lessons learned. They then prepare a list of suggestions for their own new assignment for the next group.

Conferences And Seminars

Attending professional seminars, luncheon speeches, or conferences is a good way to keep up-to-date on current topics. There is considerable expense involved in sending someone to these events or to a conference in another city or state.

As a manager, you ensure a greater return on this investment by following these suggestions:

☐ Set goals and discuss expectations with the staff member who will attend.

☐ Ask the staff member to plan a presentation for the department upon return. It can highlight new information and ideas, report on work of other organizations, and recommend action for the work group or organization.

☐ Request a brief, written conference report for distribution, discussion, and action.

CONFERENCE REPORT FORM

Name: _____

Conference title: _____

Conference Sponsor: _____

Conference dates/place:_____

Overall evaluation of conference:

_____

_____

Ideas for future planning:

_____

_____

Immediate application to our work:

_____

_____

New resources identified *(e.g., books, videos, software, etc.)*:

_____

_____

Follow-through activities or discussions recommended:

_____

_____

Occasionally managers arrange to send everyone in the section or department to a special public seminar. Goal setting and planning prior to the session, combined with a post-seminar group meeting, contribute to making the results last. One manager booked a conference room at the seminar hotel location and organized refreshments for his staff immediately following the seminar. During this informal meeting, the staff discussed the speaker's presentation and planned specific ways to follow-through together. Because everyone scheduled this discussion and planning time, they were prepared to contribute ideas and take action.

Team-Building Days

Sometimes departments set aside a day for renewing the energy and motivation of the team. Called team-building, these events are usually facilitated by someone outside the department. Planning, preparation, and an agenda that includes time for follow-through discussions make the difference between average events and excellent ones.

One Mountain Health training facilitator designed a worksheet that outlined the various team-building activities of the day. Three times during the day, participants used the worksheet on the following page for discussion and goal setting.

LESSONS LEARNED: A GUIDE FOR PERSONAL TRAINING FOLLOW-THROUGH

Activities and Lessons Learned

Consider the team-building activities, presentations, and small group discussions presented today. Think about actions and goals to bring back to the Home Health Care Division.

1. Horse Trade Activity
   I plan to:

2. Myers-Briggs Type Indicator
   I will try:

3. Hollow Squares Exercise
   I must:

4. Ron's presentation and small-group discussion questions
   Two or three specific goals:

   One behavior to eliminate:

   One communication idea:

   One idea for follow-through:

5. Goal Posting
   I plan to:

Off-The-Shelf Training Packages

Sometimes the purchase of a predesigned training program is a cost-effective answer to a training challenge.

In these cases, preview the program, watch the video, examine the workbook materials, and prepare the participants. It is critical to add your own post-training assignment or practice activities. Avoid the tendency to forget follow-through for off-the-shelf packages by considering these suggestions:

❏ Before purchase, compare training packages to find the one that addresses your needs and on-the-job applications.

❏ Modify the package (e.g., add goal setting, practice, and feedback time).

❏ If the program lasts three hours or longer, offer it in two parts to allow for practice between sessions.

❏ Require an assignment that will reinforce your department's objectives for the training program. Let the trainees know this assignment in advance so that they will expect some benefit from the practice.

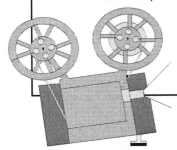

MORE FOLLOW-THROUGH TOOLS AND TIPS

Designing new and interesting follow-through training assignments that ensure practice and application tap Helene and Kami's creativity. Here are unique, fun, and innovative tools that will inspire you to design your own. Use these bold moves alone or in combination with others.

Job aids

Make small, portable, and laminated index card size reminders for telephone skills or customer service scripts. Place within easy sight.

Awards

Have trainees nominate the coworker who does the best at the new skill or behavior after one month. Meet informally to present the award and review the training ideas.

Symbols

Choose a symbol of the new attitude, behavior, or skill and place it by your phone, work station, or computer to remind you to act. Draw the symbol on a card, if necessary, or use a photograph.

Partner

Select someone in the workshop or course to meet with or phone regularly. Seek and offer feedback and support to each other.

Journal

Take five minutes daily to record your successes and lessons learned in a notebook. Set new goals based on your reflection.

Video

At the end of your training program, record a short video of yourself or your team. Encourage yourself to apply and practice the new skills. Give yourself goals. Motivate! Decide what you want of yourself or your team over a specified period of time. Watch the video at that time, and perhaps two or three months later, and see how well you did.

Record and review a complete meeting or a short segment of one. Critique your group dynamics and set new goals. If a video is impractical, use a portable audiotape recorder.

Audio

 Use a microcassette tape recorder to keep an audio journal for yourself and/or your coach. Use an audiotape to record questions as they come up.

Mail

Write yourself a letter or postcard about a goal you want to accomplish. List several benefits for yourself. Have the training facilitator mail this back to you at a certain time to remind you of the goal and encourage your progress.

E-mail

 Put key forms, check sheets, meeting agenda template, or other print tools introduced in the workshop on-line for everyone to use easily. Use E-mail to remind trainees of goals, recognize successes, and encourage new behaviors.

Learning contract

In advance of longer training programs, have trainees complete a simple learning contract that lists benefits, goals, and measures. Review and revise the contract at the end of the program. Revisit it again after three months.

Panel

Three or four weeks after the training course, have a lunchtime panel of trainees discuss their successes and lessons learned. Announce this event in all the course materials so that participants schedule and prepare for it.

Retest or reassess

If you used some kind of assessment instrument at the beginning of the workshop or course, set a date for the retest and publish the results and averages, or provide the data privately along with some coaching. For example, a safety workshop facilitator who uses a self-assessment of personal safety practices issues the same assessment three months later. Trainees complete the same questions and note their improvement.

Get real; solve a problem

Nothing has more lasting effect than to apply new concepts and methods to a real problem.

Become a coach

There is no better way to follow-through on new skills than having to teach, demonstrate, or coach someone else.

CHAPTER TEN

SUMMARY

The real work begins after the training program ends. Yet post-training coaching and follow-through present challenges—and rewards—of their own.

Most organizations spend considerable time and money on the presentation of training information, but give little attention to practice or implementation. Like the newest fad diet, organizations seem willing to pay for the nutritional advice but fail to eat differently or exercise. They waste precious time, effort, and training dollars.

The tools, practice suggestions, and examples from Arrow Computer and Mountain Health demonstrate what it takes to apply newly learned skills in the everyday business world. Before, during, and after the training program, managers, training specialists, and the trainees must think about what it will take to make follow-through happen.

Trainees will always need to acquire new technical skills, improve their communication techniques, and learn new business and management tools. Before deciding to train, managers must also ask themselves if they are ready to commit the time to make whatever changes are needed to support newly learned behaviors. They need to coach and motivate trainees after a program by reminding them of goals and benefits, and by recognizing and rewarding their efforts to apply new skills.

Rethink training in your organization. Give post-training activities more attention using the methods and tools of *Make Your Training Results Last*. It will double the impact of your training investment.

Organizations create learning cultures and environments where the line between classroom training and the real work environment becomes less distinct. Follow-through! Make your training take root!

REPRODUCIBLE FORMS AND WORKSHEETS

The pages in the Appendix are provided for you to photocopy and use appropriately.

ACTIVITY ANALYSIS
FOR TRAINING SPECIALISTS

Use a form containing items similar to these to prepare for follow-through activities. Complete one form for each major activity, exercise, or unit of the training program. *(A three-hour workshop might require two to six forms.)*

Prior to *(preferably)* or immediately following the training program, review these forms with the trainees' manager.

Training Program: _____

Presented by:_____

Developer/Writer:_____

Presentation date:_____

1. Training activity, event, or unit, and time spent in this activity:

_____

_____

2. Planned outcome of activity *(what is produced, learned, etc.):*

_____

_____

_____

_____

_____

3. How, when, or under what conditions will the new skill or information developed in this activity occur on the job?

_____

_____

_____

_____

4. Ideas for on-the-job practice or application activities:

_____

_____

_____

_____

5. Feedback on practice or application: What should the manager or training specialist observe in the practice? What form should their feedback take?

_____

_____

_____

_____

6. Additional resources required to build skills or improve pratice:

_____

_____

_____

PREPARATION CHECKLIST

GENERAL STEPS	SPECIFIC STEPS
For Managers...	
❒ Decide or clarify how the training will benefit his/her people improve their performance, and support the department's objectives.	
❒ Communicate expectations and goals for the training session. Seek staff needs and interests.	
❒ Plan time for follow-through practice and feedback activities to reinforce new or changed behaviors.	
❒ Provide input to the training design, as requested. Offer ideas for follow-through.	
For Training Staff...	
❒ Follow good training development practices.	
❒ View the trainees' manager as an important internal customer who is critical to the success of the follow-through.	
For Trainees...	
❒ Know the purpose for the training and identify several personal benefits.	
❒ Request and review the training agenda. Complete the requested prework.	

IDENTIFYING FOLLOW-THROUGH OPPORTUNITIES

Use this worksheet as you review a proposed training program to ensure training follow-through.

Is this type of event or activity found in the program? If not, could it be added or could a planned activity be modified?

❑ Videos that present situations and styles the participants relate to, and can recall and visualize later

❑ Activity debriefs *(reviews)* and discussions that help the trainees pull new ideas together, summarize what they have learned, and take the ideas away from the course

❑ Small-group activities that allow trainees from the same work unit to build a basis for strong follow-through tasks

❑ Training materials that summarize key content and prompt trainees to plan for actions they will need to take post-training

❑ *(If the program is more than several hours)* Multiple sessions that offer a progressive series of projects or assignments to be accomplished between sessions

❑ Time for practice activities within the training session

❑ Time for clarification and discussion during the program

❑ Instructor modeling of new behaviors

❑ Post-program assignments and goal setting

PERSONAL LEARNING CONTRACT

1. Outcome

What major area of improvement *(habit, skill)* in *(topic or subject area)* will I address over the next three months?

_____

_____

What specifically do I want? What is the goal?

_____

_____

2. Importance

How do I know that this is an important area for me?

_____

_____

3. Context

When and in what circumstances do I want to be able to demonstrate new skills?

_____

_____

4. Indicators

How will I know that I have achieved my goals?

_____

_____

How will my manager know?

_____

_____

5. Benefits
What are the benefits or advantages to me in doing this?

_____

_____

What difference will the outcome make in the quality of my life?

_____

_____

6. Barriers
Up until now, what has kept me from doing this? What people, places, things, or events might make it difficult for me?

_____

_____

7. Support
What resources do I have to achieve the goal? Who will provide me feedback?

_____

_____

_____

LESSONS LEARNED WORKSHEET:
A GUIDE FOR PERSONAL TRAINING
FOLLOW-THROUGH

Activities and Lessons Learned

1. Based on team-building activities, presentations, and small group discussions presented during the training, list important activities from training programs.

_____

_____

_____

_____

_____

_____

_____

_____

_____

_____

_____

_____

2. List planned actions or goals using starter phrases such as:

- I plan to…
- I will…
- I must…

Specific goals include…

	I will:	
• A communication idea…	• eliminate…	• increase…
• A follow-through idea…	• add…	• focus…
• Help I need…	• expand…	• reduce…

_____

_____

_____

_____

_____

_____

_____

_____

_____

_____

_____

POST-TRAINING CHECKLIST	
GENERAL STEPS	**SPECIFIC STEPS**
For Managers... ❏ Provide an application assignment immediately following the program. ❏ Communicate the follow-through plan. Monitor and measure progress. ❏ Implement an action plan to reduce workplace barriers that make it difficult to adopt newly learned behaviors. ❏ Reinforce improved performance and change.	
For Training Staff... ❏ Be available and offer support. ❏ Assist with data collection. ❏ Observe results, and recognize good efforts on everyone's part. ❏ Complete a thorough course evaluation.	
For Trainees... ❏ Ask for feedback from your manager and peers. ❏ Communicate ongoing needs to training staff and your manager.	

EVALUATING VENDOR /CONSULTANT FOLLOW-THROUGH

PROGRAM:_____

VENDOR:_____

Review training materials

1. Do the in-session training activities *(i.e., small-group discussions, activity debriefs, workbook materials)* address needs for follow-through?

_____

_____

2. Does the program allow time for practice and goal setting?

_____

_____

3. Are the practice assignments relevant, challenging, and realistic in scope?

_____

_____

When checking references, ask:

Did the programs developed or provided by the vendor/consultant include follow-through? If not, why not?

How did the vendor/consultant help the trainees and the managers prepare for the training?

How did the vendor/consultant demonstrate an interest in the trainees' results—one, two, and three months after the program?

THE PRACTICAL GUIDEBOOK COLLECTION FROM RICHARD CHANG ASSOCIATES, INC. PUBLICATIONS DIVISION

Our Practical Guidebook Collection is growing to meet the challenges of the ever-changing workplace of the 90's. Available through Richard Chang Associates, Inc., fine bookstores, training and organizational development resource catalogs and distributed internationally.

QUALITY IMPROVEMENT SERIES

- Meetings That Work!
- Continuous Improvement Tools Volume 1
- Continuous Improvement Tools Volume 2
- Step-By-Step Problem Solving
- Satisfying Internal Customers First!
- Continuous Process Improvement
- Improving Through Benchmarking
- Succeeding As A Self-Managed Team
- Process Reengineering In Action
- Measuring Organizational Improvement Impact

MANAGEMENT SKILLS SERIES

- Coaching Through Effective Feedback
- Expanding Leadership Impact
- Mastering Change Management
- On-The-Job Orientation And Training
- Re-Creating Teams During Transitions

HIGH PERFORMANCE TEAM SERIES

- Success Through Teamwork
- Team Decision-Making Techniques
- Measuring Team Performance
- Building A Dynamic Team

HIGH-IMPACT TRAINING SERIES

- Creating High-Impact Training
- Identifying Targeted Training Needs
- Mapping A Winning Training Approach
- Producing High-Impact Learning Tools
- Applying Successful Training Techniques
- Measuring The Impact Of Training
- Make Your Training Results Last

WORKPLACE DIVERSITY SERIES

- Capitalizing On Workplace Diversity
- Successful Staffing In A Diverse Workplace
- Team-Building For Diverse Work Groups
- Communicating In A Diverse Workplace
- Tools For Valuing Diversity
- Sexual Orientation And The Workplace

ADDITIONAL RESOURCES
FROM RICHARD CHANG ASSOCIATES, INC.

Improve your training sessions and seminars with the ideal tools—videos from Richard Chang Associates, Inc. You and your team will easily relate to the portrayals of real-life workplace situations. You can apply our innovative techniques to your own situations for immediate results.

TRAINING VIDEOTAPES

Mastering Change Management*
Turning Obstacles Into Opportunities

Step-By-Step Problem Solving*
A Practical Approach To Solving Problems On The Job

Quality: You Don't Have To Be Sick To Get Better**
Individuals Do Make a Difference

Achieving Results Through Quality Improvement**

*Authored by Dr. Richard Chang and produced by Double Vision Studios.
**Produced by American Media Inc. in conjunction with Richard Chang Associates, Inc.
  Each video includes a Facilitator's Guide.

"THE HUMAN EDGE SERIES" VIDEOTAPES

Total Quality: Myths, Methods, Or Miracles
Featuring Drs. Ken Blanchard and Richard Chang

Empowering The Quality Effort
Featuring Drs. Ken Blanchard and Richard Chang

Produced by Double Vision Studios.

"THE TOTAL QUALITY SERIES"
TRAINING VIDEOTAPES AND WORKBOOKS

Building Commitment *(Telly Award Winner)*
How To Build Greater Commitment To Your TQ Efforts

Teaming Up
How To Successfully Participate On Quality-Improvement Teams

Applied Problem Solving
How To Solve Problems As An Individual Or On A Team

Self-Directed Evaluation
How To Establish Feedback Methods To Self-Monitor Improvements

Authored by Dr. Richard Chang and produced by Double Vision Studios, each videotape from *"The Total Quality Series"* includes a *Facilitator's Guide* and five *Participant Workbooks* with each purchase. Additional *Participant Workbooks* are available for purchase.

EVALUATION AND FEEDBACK FORM

We need your help to continuously improve the quality of the resources provided through the Richard Chang Associates, Inc., Publications Division. We would greatly appreciate your input and suggestions regarding this particular guidebook, as well as future guidebook interests.

Please photocopy this form before completing it, since other readers may use this guidebook. Thank you in advance for your feedback.

Guidebook Title: _____

1. Overall, how would you rate your *level of satisfaction* with this guidebook? Please circle your response.

   Extremely Dissatisfied   Satisfied   Extremely Satisfied

       1   2   3   4   5

2. What specific *concepts or methods* did you find <u>most</u> helpful?

   _____

   _____

3. What specific *concepts or methods* did you find <u>least</u> helpful?

   _____

   _____

4. As an individual who may purchase additional guidebooks in the future, what *characteristics/features/benefits* are most important to you in making a decision to purchase a guidebook *(or another similar book)*?

   _____

   _____

5. What additional *subject matter/topic areas* would you like to see available as a guidebook in the future?

   _____

   _____

Name *(optional):* _____

Address: _____

C/S/Z: _____   **Phone (   )** _____

PLEASE FAX YOUR RESPONSES TO: (714) 756-0853
OR CALL US AT: 1-800-756-8096